Where community and productivity meet.
- The Office, Media, PA

Your workspace community.
- Cube Space, Portland

A shared environment for working and collaboration.
- Berkeley Coworking, Berkeley

Individuality without isolation.
- Office Nomads, Seattle

This is the way Philly does coworking.
- Independents Hall, Philadelphia

Smart people work here.
- Work Space, Vancouver

Work wide open.
- BlankSpaces, Los Angeles

I'm Outta Here!

How coworking is making the office obsolete

Drew Jones   Todd Sundsted   Tony Bacigalupo

Not an MBA Press
Brooklyn • Austin

Published by Not an MBA Press.

1309 E. 7th Street
Austin, TX 78702
(512) 506-1329

http://NotAnMBA.com
AKA@NotAnMBA.com

First Published 2009.

Cover design by Tony Bacigalupo.
Cover photo by Flickr user rahims: http://tr.im/iohcover
Used under a Creative Commons license: http://tr.im/iohcovercc

First edition.

Acknowledgments

Drew thanks his family—Jean, Mae, Stuart and Christopher—for understanding his long absences and endless phone calls.

Todd sends his love to Tracy, Sam and Katie. This project took far more time than planned, but their support never waned.

Tony thanks his family, Carolyn, and House 2.0 for their love and support, and Desktop Solutions, Amit, Sanford, Alex, Tara, Chris, and everyone in the Coworking movement for giving him the chance to be part of an incredible community.

From all of us go thanks to coworkers around the world for sharing your stories, ideas and time with us. This book would not exist without you.

Finally, thanks to Charlene Jaszewski, who came along at the last minute and provided invaluable editing and literary guidance to the project. Charlene saved us from ourselves and proved that expert editing does matter!

Contents

Introduction

If you endure the twice-daily rush-hour commute to an office, you probably like the idea of working from home. You gain convenience, flexibility, and autonomy. The work gets done. Everyone wins.

But many times, working from home means working alone, and working alone means losing human interaction, support, structure, and often balance.

Working alone and remaining productive and happy is a day-to-day challenge for many corporate teleworkers and over ten million freelance professionals (programmers, designers, writers, and others) throughout the United States.

Welcome to Coworking

What if you could combine the best parts of an office environment—community, collaboration, and access to the right tools—with the benefits of working at home or working for yourself—convenience, flexibility, autonomy? Imagine an office environment minus the cube farm, the hierarchy, and the politics, where individuals and small teams work alongside peers who work for other companies.

Impossible, you say?

Places like this exist today. These places are called coworking spaces.

There are many flavors of coworking—from ad hoc work-togethers called Jellies to dedicated spaces where freelancers rent a desk, to live/work arrangements.

Right now, there are over 70 coworking spaces up and running worldwide—and the number continues to grow at a rapid pace. There are Jelly groups in over 30 cities in the US, Europe, Asia, and Africa.

Many of the people who work in coworking spaces are independent freelancers or members of small (one to three person) businesses. Other coworkers work for large companies.

We spent the past year visiting coworking spaces and Jelly groups, and have gotten involved along the way. One of the authors is a member of a coworking space (Conjunctured Coworking in Austin, Texas), one of the authors founded a Jelly group (in Birmingham, Alabama) and another just opened a coworking space (New Work City in New York City). We want to spread the word about coworking because we believe it is an important movement—a symbol of much larger and exciting changes taking place in the world of work.

Industrial Age assumptions about the where, when, who and even why of work are shifting as a new generation enters the workplace. Coworking embodies and articulates these changes perfectly.

Corporate Values

- We are your employer.
- You will come to the office.
- You will stay in your cube.
- Talking to other coworkers is distracting you from your work.
- You will work on whatever project we put in front of you.
- You will put in face time so I know you are working and not screwing around.
- Your work and your life outside work are separate.

Coworking Values

- You are my client.
- I will set my own hours.
- I will work where it fits me best.
- Talking to other people energizes my work, helps me collaborate and solve problems, and is essential for my social well-being.
- I will work on projects that are meaningful to me.
- I will work until the project is completed.
- My work and my life are intertwined.

The Book

The book is laid out in six sections.

In the first section, we introduce coworking and talk about the Coworking movement and Jelly.

The second section tells stories about points in the history of the work-collectives and the beginnings of coworking itself. The third section is about the people we met along the way and the projects they're working on. Many of these stories demonstrate the incredible energy that people put into projects they are passionate about. In the fourth section, we take the reader on a tour of coworking spaces we've visited in the United States and elsewhere.

In the fifth section, we talk about companies that are innovating around work in ways that parallel coworking. And finally, in the sixth section, we explore what all of this means for work in the future.

In writing this book, we limited ourselves to stories about the places we visited and the people we personally met or talked to. We recognize that there are omissions, as there will be in projects of this scope, and we apologize in advance to those people we didn't include. Leave feedback for us on our site, http://imouttaherethebook.com, and help us make the next version better!

Researching this book has been an eye-opening experience, and we're eager to share the experience with you. Enjoy!

What is Coworking?

In this section, we introduce the concept of coworking and explain how it relates to the movement of the same name, as well as to Jelly's casual work-togethers.

The Word "Coworking"

The word "coworking" means different things to different people. People use it as:

- **A proper noun to describe a movement**
  "The core values of Coworking are..."
- **A verb to describe an activity**
  "I'm coworking with my friends at the local cafe."
- **An adjective to describe a space**
  "Souk is a coworking space in Portland."

While the Coworking movement has a specific set of core values, many have generalized the word to describe the activity.

A Movement Begins

"Traditionally, society forces us to choose between working at home for ourselves or working at an office for a company. If we work at a traditional 9 to 5 company job, we get community and structure, but lose freedom and the ability to control our own lives. If we work for ourselves at home, we gain independence but suffer loneliness and bad habits from not being surrounded by a work community.

"Coworking is a solution to this problem. In coworking, independent writers, programmers, and creators come together in community a few days a week. Coworking provides the office of a traditional corporate job, but in a very unique way."

Brad Neuberg, August 2005

Some Get It

Polly LaBarre, business writer and former editor of Fast Company magazine, visited Jelly in NYC this spring on assignment from CNN Business. Her CNN report in 2008 was one of the first nationally broadcast stories on coworking:

"Coworking is the best of both worlds. You have the collegiality and the collaboration of the office space without the politics, you have the coffee and the mix of ideas and the informality of the coffee shop without having to fight for an electrical outlet at Starbucks, and you have all the freedom and flexibility of working at home. So these sites have popped up all over the world in the last two years."

Polly got it. Her co-host was not quite up to speed:

"It's all very kinda 1960's, isn't it? I saw something like that in Washington! At George Washington University the other day, there's a bunch of frat house guys that were doing landscaping out front, listening to Led Zeppelin with a bong displayed prominently on the table in front of them! I mean, are we going back in time here?"

Photo by Todd Sundsted

Jelly Anyone?

In early 2006, entrepreneurs Amit Gupta and Luke Crawford invited their friends to come over and work from their Manhattan apartment (known as House 2.0). They christened the work-together sessions "Jelly" and two and a half years later, Jelly in Manhattan still meets at House 2.0.

Meanwhile, Jelly spread outward from New York City. At last count, there are active communities in over 30 cities worldwide.

Sometimes people connect with others to bid for projects; sometimes they simply connect and talk shop about a programming language or tool. Totally free and voluntary, hosted at coffee shops and apartments, these *ad hoc* work communities spread like a global wildfire.

You're Supposed to be Interrupted

During lunch with Amit Gupta at the wifi-cafe-laundromat BrainWash in San Francisco, we asked him if he sees any differences between Coworking and Jelly. It's an important question because Jelly has been labeled "casual coworking."

Amit suggested that Jelly is less of a continuous community than coworking is. In a coworking space, people often work in the same place on a regular basis and develop lasting friendships and connections. By contrast, according to Amit:

> People come to Jelly for the purpose of working alongside others, sharing ideas, and meeting new people—it's much more interactive and concentrated in that respect because people come with the intent to interact.
>
> Coworking spaces foster connection over a longer period of time.
>
> **Amit Gupta**

When asked about the problem of being interrupted while working at a Jelly, Amit insists: "You're supposed to be interrupted—that's what it is about."

Formulating a Coworking Recipe

Citizen Space, one of the earliest coworking spaces, offers five core values of coworking that many other spaces have adopted and used as a coworking recipe:

- 1 part - Community
- 1 part - Openness
- 1 part - Collaboration
- 1 part - Sustainability
- 1 part - Accessibility

Start with community. Blend like-minded people of different backgrounds together thoroughly. Add openness. Share ideas, thoughts, knowledge and problems in equal parts. Sprinkle collaboration on top. Ingredients will meld together to create new flavor. Add healthy amounts of sustainability. This will help maintain the recipe's structure and prevent it from falling apart. Wrap in accessibility. Make sure all ingredients are given proper opportunity to interact. Enjoy!

"Jelly is the Gateway Drug to Coworking"

"So anyone can come to Jelly?"

"Yes."

"But I don't know anybody. Is that okay?"

"Yes."

"So I show up with my laptop, and sit in your living room, and work for free."

"Yes."

"Is this as awesome as it looks?"

"Yes!"

The Roots of Coworking

Coworking has its roots in the artisan colonies and collectives of the past—organizations and spaces that existed to support the work of their members, many of whom worked alone.

This chapter takes a look at the historical context of work communities, and some of the early forays into coworking.

La Ruche

At the turn of the century, artists from around the world came to live and work in Paris. Upon arrival, many made for La Ruche.

La Ruche is in Montparnasse, which at the time was the heart of artistic life in Paris. It was originally a temporary structure created by Gustave Eiffel for the Paris Exposition of 1900. Alfred Boucher, a successful sculptor, reassembled the building at its current location in 1902 and created a **live/work space** for artists.

La Ruche met two needs for its residents. It was a community space that cut across traditional boundaries like nationality and religion/creed, and it became a community of peers that centered on the work of its residents.

The Writers Room

While many American workers traded blue collars for white collars and moved from factory floors to cube farms in the 20th century, writers continued to create value largely on their own.

The Writers Room is, as its name indicates, a shared space for writers. It was founded as a non-profit by a group of writers in New York City in 1978, and hosts up to 40 writers at a time, 24 hours a day, 365 days a year.

What do these writers produce?

> ...in 2006 there were more than four dozen fiction and non-fiction publications and several films optioned and plays by writers put into production.

writersroom.org

The San Francisco Writers' Grotto

The original hypothesis—that community is conducive to productivity—has proven abundantly true. In the past twelve years a steady stream of books, articles, feature films, television series, short stories, poems and essays has had their genesis here.

Early misconceptions were that the Grotto was a clubhouse or bohemian retreat, not a place where artists welcomed the discipline of structuring their work lives, and building a community of peers.

sfgrotto.org

Po Bronson, Ethan Watters and Ethan Canin founded the San Francisco Writers' Grotto in 1994. Located in downtown San Francisco at Second and Bryant streets, the Writers' Grotto provides workspace for about 30 writers, who engage in everything from poetry to journalism.

Proto-Coworking at Electronic Hollywood

Coworking is more than a buzz word; it's a concept that represents a solution to a set of needs—needs that have existed for some time.

In late-1990's Silicon Alley, Jamie Levy and her company Electronic Hollywood found themselves with space to spare. She bought a long table and chairs and let independents sublet space to work alongside Electronic Hollywood.

It was a temporary response to the real estate challenges of the city at the time, but it presaged the rise of similar spaces ten years later.

John McGann and Nutopia

John McGann has been ahead of the curve for a long time. Seriously. He has a three letter domain name (jdm.com).

He was also a member at Electronic Hollywood where he sublet space from Jamie Levy, and has been running flexible workspaces of his own since 1999.

John runs Nutopia in New York City. It is home to small companies, independents, and startups. John is nonchalant about the whole thing, but he's helping foster business and entrepreneurship in a city whose entrepreneurs need space and infrastructure.

Gate 3 Work Club

> Coworking is a social movement, rather than a business model. I anticipated that there would be a grassroots movement, along with other models.
>
> **Neil Goldberg**

In 2004, Neil Goldberg, designer and founder of Praxis Product Design in the San Francisco Bay area, opened up Gate 3 Work Club in 18,000 sq. ft. of space he leased in Emeryville. An industrial designer by training, Neil observed the changing patterns of work and workplace and introduced a concept called the "work club".

Gate 3 shut down after six months of operation. The problem? Neil admits that not enough resources were dedicated to marketing and that early feedback led him to underestimate the time it would take to get to break-even.

SWAT

SWAT stands for Solos Working Alone Together.

Around the same time that Amit Gupta and Luke Crawford were cooking up Jelly in the living room of House 2.0 in NYC, Shannon Clark was cooking up something very similar in Chicago:

"The idea, which I think and hope will expand beyond Chicago, is for independent consultants and entrepreneurs to select a specific place and days. We then agree that whenever possible, we'll work from that space on those days.

"It gives us a chance to grab lunch, or share a coffee with interesting people, while also getting our work accomplished. Currently here in Evanston my friend Jack Vinson and a few others have been joining me on Tuesdays and Thursdays at Cafe Mud. If you are in town, feel free to join us there as well."

SWAT didn't expand beyond Chicago, although its close cousin, Jelly, did.

Cream Cheese

When Jelly spread from NYC outward, sympathetic spirits in other cities picked up the vibe and ran with it.

One such spirit was Alex Hillman in Philadelphia. Alex was already aware of coworking, having heard about it in mid-2006. To build up to establishing a dedicated coworking space for Philadelphia independents, Alex and crew cooked up the idea of hosting a similar semi-regular work-together, *a la* Jelly and SWAT, both of which were still new at the time.

Philly pride being what it was, the guys decided to give it a name of their own. Drawing on their collective Philadelphia heritage, and their propensity for pun-making, they dubbed the get-togethers Cream Cheese Sessions.

Jelly spawned a whole new spread.

RITUAL WORKING

Photo of Ritual Coffee Roasters http://flickr.com/photos/slayeh/
Image of Ritual Working logo http://www.flickr.com/photos/factoryjoe/

Ritual Roasters

Perhaps one of the most well known independent coffee shops in the world, Ritual Coffee Roasters in San Francisco may have been the launch pad for more startups than any other coffee shop on the planet. The folks behind Flickr, Netflix and Hot or Not were known to hold meetings there.

Its clientele is a mix of beatnik and Larry Page wannabes.

But no power outlets anywhere! This limits would-be start up billionaires from mooching wifi all day.

Ritual Roasters' distinctive iconography inspired the logo used for the Coworking Google Group. According to Tara Hunt, plans were initially laid to open a coworking space adjacent to Ritual Roasters. The name? Ritual Working.

The New Artisan Economy

The next ten years will see a re-emergence of artisans as an economic force.

Intuit Future of Small Business Report, Third Installment: The New Artisan Economy

In the 21st century, the definition of "artisan" is changing. New artisans now include designers, software developers and other kinds of technologists and creatives.

The number of independent (no-employee) businesses in the US grew from 15.5 million to 20.7 million in the ten years from 1997 to 2006. That's an average of a little over 500,000 new independent businesses each year.

Some call it the re-birth of an artisan economy, where creative, independent entrepreneurs drive economic growth.

Who's Coworking?

People and their projects are the real stars of coworking.

In this chapter we'll meet some of the influential figures in the Coworking movement, coworking space owners, and community members—people who take advantage of the camaraderie, inspiration, and opportunities for collaboration that coworking offers.

Tara Hunt

Few figures have been more prominent in the Coworking movement than Tara Hunt. Tara was an early member of San Francisco's Hat Factory and, with business partner Chris Messina, opened Citizen Space in 2006.

Since then, she's been offering advice and support to people new to coworking both on the Coworking Google Group and in person. Her contributions helped shape the community-accepted core values of coworking—Community, Openness, Collaboration, Sustainability, and Accessibility—which have guided new coworking communities to better embrace coworking as a uniform concept.

While continuing to run Citizen Space, Tara is also writing a book on social capital, organizing events, and traveling for speaking engagements, among other things.

Copyright Lane Hartwell. Used with permission from Tara Hunt.

Chris Messina

Chris Messina is an active Open Source advocate and contributor. In addition to his contributions to Microformats, OpenID, and OAuth, Chris applies Open Source values to social endeavors.

Chris was an early member of and helped run the Hat Factory, where he and Tara hatched the idea that would become Citizen Space. Chris and Tara put together a wiki, an open-invitation blog, and used a Google Group to make it easy for people to gather to learn about the Coworking concept and share their thoughts and ideas.

Chris also started BarCamp, which is an unconference where the people who attend create the agenda. He started BarCamp in response to Tim O'Reilly's FooCamp, which was criticized for its exclusiveness. BarCamps now run in cities all over the world.

The two were complimentary. BarCamp attendees loved the coworking concept and helped spread it. According to Chris, if not for BarCamp, coworking might not have taken off as it did.

Photo by Tara Hunt

37

Geek Entertainment TV

Eddie Codel is coworker-in-residence at the Hat Factory, a live/work coworking space near Potrero Hill in San Francisco.

Eddie Codel makes pixels move across the tubes. He's cofounder of Geek Entertainment TV, which covers stuff that appeals to geeks.

Like David Hasselhoff and Hoffspace. Yeah!

As Eddie talked to us about his business and about the evening and weekend meetup events held at the Hat Factory, it became clear how important web video is right now in the Bay Area.

He brought up the concept of a video-edit salon, and likened it to the French literary salons of the 18th and 19th centuries. Eddie described video-salons as a kind of collaborative video mashup, where filmmakers bring in material, which is then manipulated and transformed into new combinations with other filmmakers who have their own material.

Get ready for Web 3.0 to arrive streamed live via video.

These Guys are Intali-gent

The day we visited the Hat Factory, we met a couple of guys from a company called Intalio, a BPR (Business Process Reengineering) software firm with offices in Switzerland and Palo Alto. They work out of the Palo Alto office, but they live in San Francisco.

To avoid the miserable commute to the South Bay from San Francisco, these guys work a couple of days a week at the Hat Factory, buying themselves a couple of extra hours on those days to be more productive with work and life.

In their story lies an important and interesting theme in coworking: having access to workspace close to home!

Not only does this give a worker extra time by reducing the hours per week in the car (no amount of books on tape can give you that time back), it also reduces one's carbon footprint.

Imagine the impact this could have if multiplied over millions of people!

Oh, the French Guys?

We were in San Francisco, trying to find PariSoMa. We knew from our online research that PariSoMa was a coworking space, and we were at the address where it was supposed to be. But nothing on the nondescript street looked anything like a coworking space, or a storefront, or anything.

Just when we were about to give up and head back to the hotel, a door opened and a guy, heavily sedated with alcohol, stepped out with his dog. "Is this where PariSoMa is?" He gave us a confused look, not quite sure what to make of the situation. Then his face brightened and he said, "Oh, the French guys!" Yeah, the French Guys! He ran up the stairs and got Greg, who came down and let us in. PariSoMa is home to two companies, and a coworking space.

One of the companies, Faber Novel, is a French innovation and strategy consulting firm that opened an office in San Francisco, and the other is af83, a web development company that works with Faber Novel. In the spirit of community, they've opened up the space for others to come in and cowork.

Sean O'Steen

When we talked to Sean O'Steen, who runs the firm Tech Monkey Design, we learned how hard it can be for an independent entrepreneur with a family to find work/life balance.

Sean originally worked from home. While this was convenient, he found home far too noisy and chaotic a place to work.

Seeking an alternative, he tried working from coffeeshops, libraries, and other public places, but found they weren't dependable enough to run a business.

He then took a leap and rented an office of his own. With complete control over the environment, he was able to work in peace, but found it lonely.

Then he discovered coworking. At Berkeley Coworking, he found a balance that worked for him—a structured workplace, alongside his peers, but with the benefits of running his own business.

Finding work/life balance is rarely easy. Sean found balance in coworking.

http://flickr.com/photos/hyku/1082788698/

Raines Could Help

Whether you're thinking about starting a space or need help setting up the systems or want ways to prevent and avoid conflicts, advice on marketing or member selection, we have experience that can make your space more fun, more effective, happen sooner, with less work.

http://coworkingcoach.com/

When we were in San Francisco and were trying to arrange a visit to Berkeley Coworking, we could not find an email address, phone number, or any other way to make contact with the folks there. We were talking to Amit Gupta at the time. He said he thought Raines could help. Amit called Raines, Raines called Berkeley Coworking, he arranged a visit, and we spent a couple of hours there that afternoon.

Dangerously Awesome

> Indy Hall is more than a space. 32 Strawberry Street could burn down tomorrow, and it would suck, but Indy Hall, as a community, would still be here.
>
> **Alex Hillman**

Alex Hillman, cofounder of Indy Hall in Philadelphia, has energized both the coworking and entrepreneurial scene in Philly and made an impact on the greater coworking scene along the way.

In many ways, Alex is the quintessential millennial: bold, ambitious, and perfectly happy to upend the status quo wherever it's called for.

Having engineered the success of Indy Hall at age 24, Alex expanded his efforts, offering his help and wisdom on the Coworking Google Group and elsewhere and starting a micro-consulting service, Unstick.me. He is also writing a 95-part blog series called "Cluetrain-a-day 2009," inspired by the theses put forth in the 1999 book, "The Cluetrain Manifesto."

Appropriately enough, his blog is named DangerouslyAwesome.com.

http://flickr.com/photos/hyku/788565475/

45

http://flickr.com/photos/scobleizer/2247965219/

Noneck

Society is starting to move back to what it once was in the 19th Century before industrialization—there were collectives, salons, people working together to focus on their topics.

Noel "Noneck" Hidalgo

Noel Hidalgo, like many others, was sick of working from home. He learned about the Hat Factory and their loft-style coworking setup in 2006, and he and others in his community realized they could do something similar in a Brooklyn gallery space they had.

"There was a need that was not being serviced—people craved an alternative workplace. I chatted up people, had happy hours, and toured facilities. Then it came to: Are we going to do this? People waffled, but eventually came around. And now we've gone through a third generation of coworkers."

Noel spent seven months traveling the world, documenting his experiences along the way on his blog, "on the luck of seven." As he traveled from city to city, he discovered that what he found in San Francisco and was helping build in Brooklyn was happening everywhere.

Sanford Dickert

> Everyone was talking about opening a coworking space in NYC.
> I got sick of all the talking.
>
> **Sanford Dickert**

Sanford Dickert started CooperBricolage, a cafe-based coworking community. Out of that grew New Work City, and a growing group of like-minded independent workers.

In the world of "The Starfish and the Spider," Sanford is a catalyst. He got the community started, recruited people to participate and lead, and then offered help along the way as it grew.

Sanford doesn't cowork much himself; he leaves that to others. But his influence over coworking in New York City is undeniable.

Photo by Tony Bacigalupo

Cowo Milano

Lou Bacigalupo is a road warrior who's seen more than his fair share of boring hotel rooms.

So when he heard about how quickly coworking is spreading, he started getting inquisitive. Are there any coworking spaces in Hong Kong? How about Milan?

I told him to check out Cowo Milano, Milan's first coworking space and home to the design firm Monkey Business. I looked up the information and gave him directions to the space and contact information for the space's founder, Massimo Carraro, whom I had never spoken to previously.

When Lou was in town, he headed over to the space, and there was Massimo.

Lou introduced himself: "Hi, I'm Lou Bacigalupo."

Massimo, recognizing the name, immediately responded, "Do you know Tony?"

Geoff DiMasi

Co-founding Indy Hall is only one part of Geoff DiMasi's lengthy resume as a cultivator of community in the Philadelphia area.

As co-founder of the Passyunk Square Civic Association, he helped build a neighborhood volunteer-run organization focused on neighbors helping neighbors and on beautification.

As an adjunct professor at The University of the Arts, Geoff taught "Technique Studio," a class that helped teach industrial design students to be "web citizens" and to approach their work both as a user and a participant.

He's also a principal at P'unk Avenue, a development firm focused on higher education and business. This semester, P'unk Avenue is collectively teaching Geoff's "Technique Studio" class.

According to Geoff: "we're basically telling [the students] we want you to be part of the community. And we believe that there are benefits to being part of the community."

What did his former students do with their education? Three of them are now employed at P'unk Avenue.

We Don't Know His Name and We're not Completely Sure What He Does

In our hyper transparent world, it's surprising to encounter someone who's not interested in pumping up their Google hits. Or who is actively working on pushing it down. But, Jelly's open to everyone.

He goes by the name of Randall, but we're not convinced that's his real name. Other Atlanta Jellyers are doubtful as well. When he described the type of programming he does for clients, it was in that "if I tell you too much I'll have to kill you" tone of voice.

We didn't press him.

Photo by Todd Sundsted

Yelp!

When you head to a Jelly, you can't be sure what you're going to encounter or even how productive you're going to be, but you know you're in for something unexpected.

When we visited the Atlanta Jelly at the Urban Grind in west midtown, Deanna from Yelp was that something.

As a community builder for Yelp, her job centered on engaging the community, and getting people to sign up on Yelp. By 11am, she had hooked all of us—we were signed up, friending each other, and writing reviews.

In retrospect, Deanna may have been the only one to actually get any work done that day.

Northside Jelly

Every other Wednesday Atlanta's Northside Jelly meets at Tony's American Grille & Tap, in Alpharetta.

We walked in to find five or six guys spread out on three couches, working away. ESPN was projected on the wall, but no one seemed to pay attention. They were too busy working.

Kevin Bachman, the main organizer, heads up web development for a 12 person firm called Active Group. Active Group produces live streaming content for use in corporate focus groups. Like other technologists in the coworking scene, his work can be done from anywhere, so once a week he Jellies.

Greg, on another couch, works for a traditional media company that hired him to help with their web 2.0 strategy and community-focused marketing. He escapes to Jelly once a week also.

And Randall (if that's his real name) was there too. His hair was dyed green. "I'm off to Burning Man this weekend," he says, pre-empting our question about his hair.

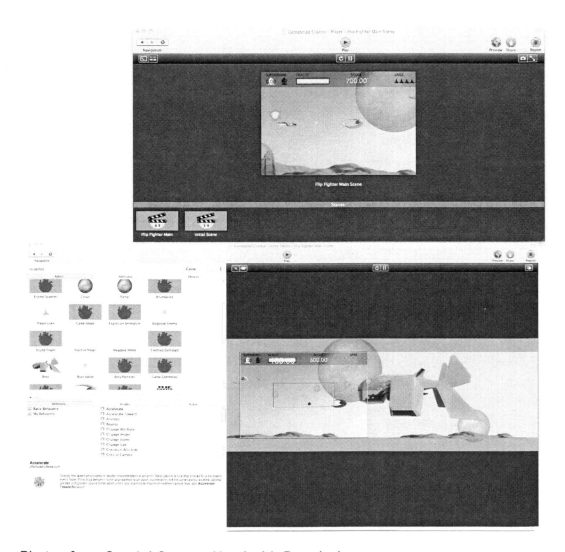

Photos from Gendai Games. Used with Permission.

Gendai Games

Conjunctured Coworking has become a hub in Austin's startup scene. In addition to its regular coworking hours during the day, Conjunctured hosts a variety of after-hours events.

In September, Gendai Games, an Austin-based game developer, held its launch party at Conjunctured. Gendai developed an application that enables non-programmers to create the rules and characters of their own video games. All four rooms of Conjunctured were full of people drinking and making their own games.

The Gendai launch drives home coworking's themes. Community, space, and friendship, as well as innovation and entrepreneurship.

Cesar Torres

When we started researching coworking, one of the first questions we wanted to ask was, "What made you decide to go into business for yourself after you graduated?" At the Jelly in Austin where we first asked that question, Cesar Torres, a very active member of the Austin coworking community and cofounder of Conjunctured, quickly pointed out that for many coworkers and young entrepreneurs the question missed the point entirely.

Cesar, along with many of his peers, started businesses while still in college. In Cesar's case, he started his first business his junior year in college, using Craigslist to find jobs that complimented his studies.

Photo by Tony Bacigalupo

Coworking is for Vaudeville Priestesses, Too

Maggie Duval and her 9 year old daughter, Hunter, who is "unschooled," write code and cowork together at Austin Jelly most Fridays.

Maggie writes software and develops web applications, but only to pay the bills. Her passion lies in a variety of other directions.

She is an ordained priest. She is editor of the Soul of an Emerging World newsletter, and an accomplished vaudeville singer.

When I asked her what it meant to her to work alongside so many like-minded people, she grew visibly excited. We traded notes about how it felt to be a part of a community at work, and at one point, she said: "It's better to not try and define it, 'cause as soon as you define it you kill it."

Obama at Conjunctured

On the last night of the 2008 Democratic National Convention, we wrapped up a day of coworking at Conjunctured in Austin. As we left, Cesar Torres, one of Conjunctured's founders, was rigging up a way to stream Obama's acceptance speech to a projector so he could watch it on one of the room's walls.

Later than night, Cesar tweeted that he got it to work and invited the community to come by to watch.

We found out later that nine people showed up, ate pizza, watched the speech, and discussed politics.

It's easy to get excited about coworking—it provides an environment in which innovation thrives. Work is clearly important, but almost as much of the creative churn in coworking revolves around life and passion outside of and complimentary to work.

best & worst   faveflow   add a site   `URL or search term` `Search`

is hiring

Psssst! See the best sites on our leaderboard.

Wearing fancy pants? You can even browse by tag.

Can't decide? Declare a draw.

39% You chose the loser.   **61%**   You voted for Peter's Dive Resort Philippines: Scuba D... **39%** agree with you.

40% You chose the loser.   **60%**   You voted for eatpoo.com. **40%** agree with you.

14%   **86%** You chose the winner!   You voted for BustedTees - Funny T-Shirts - New T-Shir.... **86%** agree with you.

From Zero to Startup in the Time it Takes to Get a Sandwich

I arrived at Jelly late. Everyone was working quietly, doing their own thing.

I left to grab a late lunch. When I returned half an hour later, the place was abuzz.

Around a dinner table, about half a dozen people were actively discussing something and typing away at their computers.

Someone had shared an idea they had for a new site, and everyone dug it.

They worked almost nonstop until 2:00 am that night. Days later, their site emerged: "Hot-or-Not for websites"—CommandShift3.

In its first month, CS3 got over one million pageviews.

A Twitter Strategy

It's August 29 and Austin Jelly is at Cafe Caffeine. Cafe Caffeine is where it all started for us.

Today a team of coworkers is filming a commercial. We asked Michelle Greer, the filmographer, what was going on.

Michelle is in charge of the Twitter Strategy for Sun and Ski, the outdoor recreation store. She has been charged with making Sun and Ski's presence on Twitter fun and, frankly, not annoying.

When some traditional companies "embrace 2.0", they simply see another opportunity to pipe in coupons, ram/jam their existing programs, and push other annoying junk. To their credit, Sun and Ski wants to be different.

So, Michelle is here at Cafe Caffeine, dressed up in ski gear, being silly, posting to Twitter, having fun. Who says business can't be fun?

Jelly—It's Not Just for Geeks

Karen Dunlap, a tea expert, founded matchasource.com, an online retailer of premium grade matcha tea and accessories. Karen was an early attendee at Jelly in NYC in 2006.

"I met a guy at a party, then checked out his website... By chance, I saw a link to Amit and his changethis.com site, then I saw a blurb about Jelly... Jelly sounded like the community I was looking for, so I took a chance and showed up with my computer."

At Jelly, Karen met with industrial designer Joey Roth to collaborate on a new teapot design. Being a solo entrepreneur and working with other independents is what attracted her to Jelly. But the place was so full of hardcore geeks she wasn't sure she was going to come back. Good thing she did.

"Somebody there [at Jelly] is an expert in just about anything that you might need information about." "Jelly gives me the confidence and energy to believe that I can succeed as an entrepreneur. It gave me the confidence to start my own blog, for example, which I would never have done on my own."

Dusty Reagan

> Consistency is a big deal in starfish organizations.
>
> **Dusty Reagan**

Dusty Reagan, owner of Floating Head Studios and co-founder of Conjunctured Coworking in Austin, TX, launched Jelly in Austin in October 2007. It is still going strong despite, or perhaps because of, the creation of new, permanent coworking spaces in Austin. According to Dusty, part of the formula is consistency.

Austin Jelly meets every Friday. It has grown to a regular turn-out of between 10 and 30, which makes it one of the largest Jellies in terms of attendees. After rotating locations for some time, Dusty and Company made the decision to host Jelly each week at Cafe Caffeine.

Now everyone knows what and where, if not who.

Photo by Todd Sundsted

Darrell Silver

Darrell Silver got into Jelly because he had Fridays off (he worked the Asian markets) and wanted to do something besides finance.

Darrell, along with Amit Gupta, Lee Semel, and Erin Sparling, conceived of the web site CommandShift3 at a Jelly hosted by Darrell toward the end of 2007. CommandShift3 is kind of like a beauty contest for web sites. As we write this, visitors have cast over 1,691,652 votes for their favorite web site designs.

Darrell and Amit are now working on JellyDesk, a platform for sharing and finding space to work.

Per Darrell, neither project would have happened if it hadn't been for Jelly.

A Gathering of the Tribes at SXSW

The South by Southwest (SXSW) Interactive Festival has emerged as a pivotal annual event for new startups and tech trends.

SXSW 2008 was coworking's coming out party. People from cities all over the country and the world convened to trade notes and share stories about their experiences.

A year's worth of online communication was made real—face to face—as coworkers from Philadelphia (Alex Hillman and Johnny Bilotta from Indy Hall), San Francisco (Eddie Codel from the Hat Factory and Tara Hunt from Citizen Space), Bryan, Texas (Cody Marx Bailey from the Creative Space), Seattle (Jacob Sayles from Office Nomads), Wausau, Wisconsin (Marcus Nelson from the now-defunct Citizen Desk), Austin (Julie Gomoll from Launchpad Coworking and Cesar Torres, Dusty Reagan, John-Erik Metcalf, and David Walker from Conjunctured) and many more gathered in one spot.

The message was clear:

Coworking is for real.

Coworking Spaces

In the few short years since the Coworking movement's inception, over 70 coworking spaces have popped up in dozens of cities worldwide. One of the only things they have in common is their sheer diversity.

Despite their differences, these spaces share a critical commonality—they're built to serve the needs of a new class of workers who require an new class of workspace.

Spiral Muse

Before the word "coworking" existed, Brad Neuberg knew he needed to find a way to bring more structure and balance to his independent work life. He consulted a life coach, Audrey Seymour, and while working with her, came up with the idea of coworking as a solution.

He set up shop in a converted Victorian house called the Spiral Muse in the Mission District of San Francisco, invited people to "cowork" with him, and offered a structured day: Arrive at 9:00am. Start with meditation. Focus on work and sharing ideas with the community next. Stop for lunch together. Schedule a 45 minute break in the afternoon for a healthy group activity. End the day at 5:45pm sharp.

For the increasing number of people who are pursuing independent careers, this kind of focus on self-imposed structure is critical to maintaining a healthy work/life balance.

Nutopia

Before the word "coworking" was used to describe the movement, John McGann was quietly experimenting with alternative workspaces in New York City.

In 1999, he opened 116 West Houston, an open, shared-workspace facility in Manhattan. More recently, he relocated to Tribeca and renamed his space Nutopia, after John Lennon's imaginary future.

Though the language used to describe his space in the early days was different than the language used now, he was providing space for independent entrepreneurs and small teams in need of an affordable place to work. That he has been at it for about a decade makes John a pioneer indeed!

http://nutopia.us

Photo by Todd Sundsted

Hat Factory

The Hat Factory, founded by coworkers from Spiral Muse in 2006, is one of the earliest coworking spaces still in operation and has inspired many spaces since.

The Hat Factory is a live-work space with three loft apartments on the top floor and a large, open space with a big table, a couch, and lounge chairs downstairs. For a place that has such widespread recognition and significance in the scene, the Hat Factory is an unassuming place.

It has three live in-residents and eight regular members. Eddie Codel, a resident-member, runs Geek Entertainment TV there. Ryan Bailey, another resident-member, runs his video community site Viddyou there as well.

Eddie and Ryan live upstairs and work downstairs. Now that's a sustainable commute!

http://hatfactory.net

Photo by Todd Sundsted

Citizen Space

The idea of Citizen Space is to take the best elements of a coffee shop (social, energetic, creative) and the best elements of a workspace (productive, functional) and combine them to give indie workers the chance to have their own, affordable space.

http://citizenspace.us

Citizen Space was an extension of Citizen Agency, a community-building and social marketing firm based in the San Francisco Bay Area. Citizen Space is something of a coworking prototype—it has largely defined the values and goals of much of the coworking movement worldwide.

That's thanks, in large part, to the fact that Chris and Tara took Brad's advice to heart: Use the idea. Remix it. Share it.

Citizen Space currently has a waiting list for membership, but is expanding to meet demand. Dropping in for the day, however, is free and open to all.

According to Tara, drop-ins provide Citizen Space with a constant flow of creative people to interact and work with.

http://citizenspace.us

Independents Hall

Its name a clever play on the nearby historical landmark, Independents Hall is a shining example of a coworking space done right. It strikes just the right balance of serious workplace, creative environment, and rebellious clubhouse, and the result is a community that's energized a city.

In short order, the talented folks at Indy Hall have produced applications, internet TV shows, micro-consulting services, and much more, and the innovation continues. Several of Indy Hall's members have joined forces to form IndyHall Labs, to catalyze and augment the ad hoc collaboration of new projects.

Founded by Alex Hillman, Geoff DiMasi, and Bart Mroz, Indy Hall has served as inspiration not just to Philadelphia but to people interested in coworking everywhere.

http://indyhall.org

http://flickr.com/photos/hyku/1726458603/

Williamsburg Coworking

Be the change you want to see in the world.

Mahatma Ghandi

Williamsburg Coworking, founded by Beka Economopoulos and Noel Hidalgo, works out of a storefront space in Brooklyn that houses The Change You Want to See Gallery. Inside you'll find examples of the kind of change we want to see: kindness, camaraderie, and fierce passion for helping make the world a better place.

In October, Williamsburg Coworking hosted a Jam Session to produce a product called Twitter Vote Report—a decentralized election monitoring system that allowed voters to use text messages to report incidents of voter suppression, long lines, broken machines, and other disruptions on election day.

It's no surprise that Twitter Vote Report, The Change You Want to See Gallery, and one of the world's first coworking spaces all appeared in Brooklyn. As a center of American culture, creativity, and independence, there is no shortage of free-minded souls unwilling to accept the status quo.

http://coworking.pbwiki.com/Coworking+Brooklyn

Photo by Tony Bacigalupo

SocialText

Good coworking spaces have a "liveness" about them. People come. People interact. People go. Sometimes the space itself comes into being, transforms itself a few times, and goes away.

The story of SocialText's foray into coworking is a perfect example of this. For about a year, roughly between February 2007 and June of 2008, SocialText, a Palo Alto-based company whose applications focus on online collaboration, took the extra space in their office and offered others an ultra-simple model: drop in; $10 suggested donation. Keep it simple.

Eventually, the SocialText business grew into the space and the coworking space was no more.

Village Quill

We would have told you stories about the people working here, or about the buzz of activity, or about the owner's thoughts—but when we toured the space, we heard one thing—silence.

To the busy writers at the Village Quill in New York City, working in a shared space alongside other writers doesn't mean chatter!

http://villagequill.com

Sandbox Suites

Sandbox Suites in San Francisco has significantly advanced the built-environment aspect of coworking. A much larger space than Hat Factory or Citizen Space, Sandbox Suites has different types of space—some for meetings, some for solo work, some for whole start-up teams, and some of the space is open, café-lounge space.

Roman Gelfer, the space's founder and manager, regularly hosts tech meetups, writers' meetups, lectures, classes, and parties.

Unlike some of the other spaces in the, which are not intended to be profit-oriented businesses, Sandbox Suites is a business that seeks to pay the salaries of its owners. Importantly, the business is being built around the community.

For those of you who've wondered "Whatever happened to MC Hammer?," as we have, wonder no longer. His company, DanceJam.com, is based at Sandbox Suites— which makes him a member of the global coworking community.

http://sandboxsuites.com

Photo by Todd Sundsted

Photo by Todd Sundsted

Berkeley Coworking

Every coworking space is different. Berkeley Coworking is a space yet to be completely defined.

Jonathan Zamick, the space's leader, has filled the place with architecturally interesting pieces—moveable partitions and rooms, whiteboards of different types, and easily constructible tables that can be used and broken down.

Jonathan previously worked with M.G. Taylor, the innovative architect known for designing creative workspaces and office furniture. He has carried some of this work with him into coworking. When we asked him what his goals were for how these pieces would be used, he was noncommittal. He does, though, clearly see coworking as an organic alternative to the large corporation. This is what Berkeley Coworking is out to create.

http://berkeleycoworking.com

Cubes & Crayons

This is not your parents' office.

Cubes & Crayons is a hybrid workspace and day care center, where parents both bring their children to work and get to spend their day alongside peers.

According to its founder, Felicity Chapman, Cubes & Crayons arose from the dual realizations that:

- People should have the flexibility to work and have kids at the same time.
- Corporations are losing a very valuable resource in men and women who have to compromise their careers in order to devote time and energy to a family.

As part of a movement that continues to explore the role work plays in our lives, Cubes & Crayons addresses a major problem plaguing the white collar world, and has found an exciting solution.

http://cubesandcrayons.com

Photos provided by Cubes & Crayons

Office Nomads

At SXSW we met Jacob Sayles, one half of the duo that put coworking on the map in Seattle at Office Nomads. Jacob and Susan Evans created a lively, well designed, community-oriented space for independents (and others) to work together.

Their tag—Individuality Without Isolation—strikes a chord with many people in the Coworking movement, and has become one of many popular slogans for coworking.

Seattle, along with Portland, San Francisco and Austin, has one of the largest populations of knowledge workers in the country who work outside of the office. That is, Seattle has lots of nomads. In the long middle months of the grey drizzle, Office Nomads is a community oasis for Seattle's nomads.

http://officenomads.com

Photo provided by Office Nomads

Photo provided by The Hive

The Hive

The Hive, in downtown Denver, opened in the repurposed basement-space of a renovated office building. Like many other coworking spaces, the Hive is a collaborative, shared-work environment combining the open atmosphere of a cafe with *work pod* areas for semi-private work.

The backstory of the Hive, though, is distinct. It is the brainchild of Andrew Luter, a Denver-based venture capitalist with BaseCamp Capital. BaseCamp invests largely in unconventional real estate plays—storage units, mobile home parks, retirement facilities, down-market resorts, and more.

To some, coworking spaces may be seen as another category of real estate.

http://hivecoop.pbwiki.com

La Cantine

La Cantine is distinctly French. It promotes a social, collective, and collaborative spirit that frankly exceeds similar goals in spaces born in America's more individualistic and competitive culture.

Funded heavily by private and public organizations in the region, La Cantine sits at the center of the Parisian tech sector known as "Silicon Sentier" (literally "Silicon Alley").

While offering both free drop-in workspace as well as paid workspace, La Cantine's main emphasis is on events.

A French friend of ours says that the best way to think of La Cantine is like a modern version of a library—a public resource, open to the people.

http://lacantine.org

Station C

We want it to be a year-long BarCamp.

Patrick Tanguay

Station C, Montreal's first coworking space, opened in the cafe-riddled neighborhood of Milend in 2008. Carefully located, designed and branded to offer just the right cultural vibe, Station C has become a hub of creative activity.

Patrick Tanguay, an inspired former member of Centre for Social Innovation, and partner Daniel Mireault described how they came up with the name in his announcement of the space's opening to the Coworking Google Group:

"We wanted something defining a zone, an area, a place in town and something bilingual so 'Station' fit the bill, we added the C for coworking of course but also community, collaboration, code, creation, citizen, center."

Too bad "awesome" doesn't start with a 'c.'

http://station-c.com

Welcome to the Scent Bubble

Le Bureau, a shared workspace facility in London's Battersea Park area, offers yet another vision of alternative workspace.

The space's founder-leader, Peter Spencer, does not use the term "coworking" to describe his business. Yet, Le Bureau incorporates many of the elements that do define coworking in other places.

Le Bureau spared nothing in terms of design detail. The chairs, desks and lamps were all designed specifically for Le Bureau. Independents and small businesses make up Le Bureau's membership base. They work in an atmosphere filled with Buddha statues, velvet meeting rooms, and an Italian-style kitchen. Perks include fresh flowers every day and a large self-serve DVD library.

In keeping with the overall experience, the air conditioning system is infused with aromatherapy oils, and the scents are misted into the space at set intervals through the day.

http://lebu.biz

Photo provided by Le Bureau

Roam Atlanta

Coworking in Atlanta has migrated to the suburbs.

Roam Atlanta is a combination café/corporate meeting space. People are free to drop in, have a coffee or lunch, and use the wifi. Roam's focus right now seems to be on the meeting rooms, which sit to the back of the space and serve a real need for suburban-based businesses looking for well-designed and inspiring off-campus meeting space.

As part of its effort to build community into its business model, Roam has recently invited the Atlanta Jelly group, which also meets in the North Atlanta suburbs, to gather in Roam's café every other Wednesday.

It is worth noting that one of Roam's founding partners is a long time IBM employee who worked remotely for over 10 years. Tired of working alone at home, he founded Roam—a place to do his work around others.

http://roamatlanta.com

The Creative Space

The Creative Space in Bryan, Texas (next to College Station, home to Texas A&M University), is a hive of activity.

- Downtown Cartel is a web development firm that has three employees and a rich pipeline of projects.
- Always Creative is a design firm—web design, communication design, print design—that sometimes does front-end work on Downtown Cartel projects.
- Activist Apparel makes t-shirts and other clothes with a social activism theme.
- Erickson Media Group is a WordPress design shop.
- Desired Hearts is community-generated fashion (a la Threadless) where a percentage of all profits go to the charity of the designer's choice.

The guys at The Creative Space are also behind BIL, the unconference and counterpoint to TED, which attracted over 500 attendees and seems poised to become a significant event with a second conference announced for 2009.

http://thecreativespace.org

Conjunctured

In July of 2008, Conjunctured Coworking opened its doors for business in a standalone craftsman-style house in East Austin. Conjunctured is the brainchild of four Austin entrepreneurs: Cesar Torres, John Erik Metcalf, Dusty Reagan, and David Walker.

Together, they make up the business collective Conjunctured LLC, a "co-company." While maintaining their respective independence, the four founders tackle projects together under the Conjunctured name. The Conjunctured workspace is a project of Conjunctured the company, which intentionally blurs the boundaries between the two.

Conjunctured has quickly become a crossroads in Austin's young entrepreneurial scene. Since they've opened they've hosted Jelly, an iPhone DevCamp, and the launch of Gendai Games, a local game startup.

http://conjunctured.com

Photo by Drew Jones

Caroline Collective

Matthew Wettergreen, a bioengineer, and Ned Dodington, an architect, brought coworking to Houston.

Caroline Collective opened in partnership with Houston-based realtor Jeff Kaplan, who saw the potential for a creative, community oriented workspace in Houston's museum district.

From the beginning, Matthew and Ned's goal was to build a space that was a part of the neighborhood, and in that respect they succeeded. The collective is the most multi-purpose space we've seen: it's a place to work, but also a place for events, for art openings, for arts and crafts nights, for film nights, and more.

Several organizations—both for profit and not for profit—base their businesses at the collective. Other areas of the space are open for individual coworking as well. Surprisingly, much of the buzz at Caroline Collective surrounds the events that the space hosts.

http://carolinecollective.cc

Ditmas Workspace

On April 1st, 2008, Liena Zagare posed a question for her neighbors in Ditmas Park, a neighborhood in Brooklyn. She wanted to know if they would be interested in "...a flexible shared office, of use to those of us who prefer working alongside others but don't have an office..."

Six months later, on September 25, 2008, she hosted an open house for Ditmas Workspace, a "shared office space for neighbors" located on the ground floor of a large Victorian house in Ditmas Park. The space used to house a physician's office and has seen both the best and the worst of New York City's changing fortunes.

The tenants include writers, editors, and other professionals, many of whom used to live and work in other parts of New York City and live and now work in Ditmas Park.

http://ditmasworkspace.com

Photo by Tony Bacigalupo

New Work City

The Manhattan real estate market is a harsh environment for the intrepid coworking pioneer. Since the coworking movement's inception, several people tried to get something off the ground in Manhattan, only to hit a wall.

So what do you do while you're looking for a space and a landlord willing to take a chance on a *movement* that's not exactly a business plan?

If you learn from New Work City's story, you work on building community: first through existing coworking groups like Jelly and Williamsburg Coworking, then by starting a new community (CooperBricolage) and using existing coffee shops. Then you recruit everyone to help. Share everything along the way.

By the time you find a space, you'll have a strong, motivated, involved group alongside you.

In its first week open for business, New Work City signed enough members to be profitable.

http://nwcny.com

LaunchPad Coworking

LaunchPad Coworking opens in 2009, and will be Austin's third coworking space to come online in the past year.

It's ironic that LaunchPad Coworking will be the last of the three coworking spaces in Austin to open its doors. The folks behind LaunchPad (principally its founder-leader Julie Gomoll) were early champions of the coworking movement in Austin, and the first to announce their intentions to open a space. Their commitment to creating a high-end, premium coworking brand, though, has evolved into full-scale business building. Launchpad will offer food and concierge services, sound-proofed media editing facilities, among other amenities.

LaunchPad Coworking will occupy a new point, at the luxury high-end, on the coworking continuum. Like London's Le Bureau, LaunchPad sets out to demonstrate that coworking is a big enough canvas to support different markets.

http://launchpadcoworking.com

Corporate Outworking

Companies are already experimenting with new models of working. These experiments include telecommuting and hoteling, combined with new management models that emphasize performance over face time.

We call this "outworking." Outworking is the process of moving work out of the office and closer to people's lives.

The fact that these companies trust their employees to work remotely is a promising first step towards a new relationship between employer and employee.

Office Productivity at Cisco

"The workplace has shifted from a heads-down, individual environment to a collaborative effort while infrastructure has become far more mobile. Workplace design was for so long shackled by the need to accommodate large physical devices in fixed locations...

"If your goal is to improve office productivity, it [mobile work] will have a profound effect due to big savings in the reduction of square footage per person. You can drive the total [space] utilization from the standard 40% to 50% or 60% and that can represent millions of dollars annually."

Mark Golan, Vice President of Connected Real Estate, Cisco
http://nreionline.com/technology/Mark_Golan

The "Future of Work" at Boeing

In 2006, Boeing launched a program called "The Future of Work." This program designated 11,000 employees as "teleworkers," who have access to any of the company's 21 hoteling stations around the country. "Hoteling" facilities are satellite offices booked by individuals and teams on an as-needed basis. No fixed desks, just space available when you need it.

Why did Boeing go down this road?

> "We want the tech-savvy to join us. We need the technical talent, because that's the future of our company. And, we need to create spaces that get them in the door.

> "How [Baby Boomers] live, how they work, and what their expectations are in terms of their work life and personal life are extremely different from the Millennials.

> "If you continue to build the kind of environments you have now, it won't be attractive to Millennials because they just don't work the same way Baby Boomers do."

http://www.buildings.com/articles/detail.aspx?contentID=3428

IBM: Virtual Company?

Almost 40% of IBM's employees have remote working status. This means no fixed-desks and no offices.

For IBM, this is a cost saving program. But it doesn't address the basic human need for social interaction. A couple of examples illustrate this point:

On one of our visits to Atlanta Jelly, we met an IBM employee who lives in Atlanta but works out of Burlington, Vermont. His wife took a job in Atlanta, so he went too. After a year of working out of his house, he grew bored and wanted to work around other people. He uses Jelly as a way to work with other people.

At Roam Atlanta, the meeting/coworking space in north Atlanta, one of the founder/owners is an IBM employee who has had remote working status for 10 years. Roam is an outgrowth of his need—developed over many years—to interact with other people.

Open Work @ Sun

While they've struggled of late, Sun Microsystems is a leader in workplace design and workforce management.

One half of their 35,000 employees participate in Sun's Open Work program, which enables employees to do their work "anytime, anywhere." Sun doesn't care if you do your work at one of Sun's offices, or on the moon. Just get it done!

All of Sun employees can enroll in Open Work. Roughly half have taken the company up on the offer.

Ann Bamesberger, Sun's Vice President of Open Work Services, says that the program saves the company around $70 million/year.

R.O.W.E. at Best Buy

What would happen if senior corporate managers evaluated employee performance on the results of their work rather than on when and where they did the work?

The executives at Best Buy, the Minneapolis based electronics and home-appliance company, sought to find out.

Led by then-employees Jody Thompson and Cali Ressler, Best Buy experimented with what they call the Results Only Work Environment (R.O.W.E.). Employees who are on R.O.W.E. teams can do their work anytime/anywhere they choose. They are evaluated on what they actually do.

For those teams at Best Buy who are on R.O.W.E., employee morale is up, employee retention is up, and employee output and productivity are up.

Jody and Cali wrote a book about it—Why Work Sucks: And How to Fix It. Their new consultancy, CultureRX, now helps other companies make the transition from face-time to results-only work.

Work/Life Revolution

Many people inside and out of the coworking community believe that real change is taking place in the world of work. In this section, we gather the thoughts of some of the people we encountered along our journey, and add some of our thoughts along the way as well.

Seven Rules of The Hedonistic Company

The German web development and design company, Zentrale Intelligence Agentur, is an un-company. They refer to themsevles as a "capitalist-socialist joint venture."

ZIA has seven unprocedures:

Rule 1
The 7 Nos - No office. No employees. No fixed costs. No pitches. No exclusivity (company doesn't own your life). No working hours (results only). No bullshit.

Rule 2
Work-Work Balance - Balance projects for clients with your passion projects, given equal priority and attention.

Rule 3
Instant Gratification - Profit immediately with work; no salaries, billable time/project, always keep 10% of profit for the company for play money; pay bills immediately as well.

Rule 4
Pluralism of Methods - Tech solutions for social problems, use online tools for collaboration; Skype, Google calendar, Google Docs.

Rule 5

Fixed Ideas - Live up to your intellectual obsessions and dark desires at work; take them seriously; don't be afraid to offend people.

Rule 6

Responsibilities Without Hierarchies - Each project has to have one person in charge, but it can be anybody; beginning of year retreat in the country; rethink the business model; sift through projects and leaders take them on.

Rule 7

The Power of Procrastination - Don't try to be too efficient; good ideas will adapt and catch on, even if you neglect them for a while; they have to ripen; there is a natural Darwinism of ideas.

Better Without Bosses

One day we sat down and decided that we didn't want to be contractors anymore. We're not trying to get permanent jobs at the places we work.

We collaborate with companies, we bring value to companies, we enjoy the money from companies, but we don't want the shackles and cubicles of companies.

But the IRS and state governments want us to be employees because big companies are easier to censure than individuals. So... are you gonna let the State get away with that?

We're here to raise consciousness. Get yourself a sticker if you agree and want to help spread the word.

We're unencumbered by employers and better without bosses. Are you?

http://NotAnEmployee.net

Accelerating Serendipity

We can sometimes be interesting people, so if we're around other interesting people, interesting things usually happen.

That's the process that we like to call accelerating serendipity. We want to be able to get really interesting people together in a space and see what kind of chemical reactions can happen.

Chris Messina, June 2007

There are several obvious benefits to coworking, but some of the best ones are those that are non-obvious. Working in a shared space with like-minded people, there's a good chance that something good will come of it. It could be that your neighbor happens to know a friend who can help, or happens to have an answer to a nagging question, or it could be that a lunchtime conversation ends up becoming a project that ends up becoming a startup.

You can't predict exactly when or how it will happen, but the potential for a happy coincidence is always present. And that's no accident.

Coworking spaces are designed to facilitate this.

3rd Axiom of Coworking

The 3rd Axiom of Coworking: many people in the coworking scene have more than one thing going on.

Over the last year we've met a lot of people who were involved with coworking, Jelly, or similar open/alternative work space projects. Toward the end of a conversation, it's customary to exchange business cards. The exchange frequently took the following form.

"I'm doing this and this," at which point they hand over a card.

"And I'm also doing this," and then another card.

Photo by Tony Bacigalupo

Passion vs. Payment

People in coworking communities tend to have a lot on their plates. Ask them what they do, and they will likely give you a list of different things they're involved in: some for money, some personal, some a combination of both.

Finding the right mix between these can be a challenge for anyone, but for independent workers it is a constant balancing act.

Some split their days between efforts, while others spend months at a time focusing on one before switching to the other.

Ultimately, this comes back to a recurring notion we've seen: balance.

By joining coworking communities, people get the chance to see and try new things, and hopefully move closer to the ideal work/life balance: doing what you love, and getting paid to do it.

The Architecture of Work/Life Balance

"The Pattern Language," by Christopher Alexander, is an inspirational book about the impact of the built environment on human relationships.

Pattern Language #9
The artificial separation of houses and work creates intolerable rifts in people's inner lives.

Pattern Language #41
If you spend eight hours of your day at work, and eight hours at home, there is no reason why your workplace should be any less of a community than your home.

Pattern Language #80
No one enjoys his work if he is a cog in a machine.

Pattern Language #82
If two parts of an office are too far apart, people will not move between them as often as they need to; and if they are more than one floor apart, there will be almost no communication between the two.

Christopher Alexander, Pattern Languages

Balance In Action

At the Spiral Muse, Brad Neuberg insisted on incorporating meditation and yoga in the course of the work day, and on knocking off at a reasonable hour so as not to overdo the work in coworking.

Sadly, this dimension of the coworking movement has largely been left behind. There are, though, a few interesting exceptions.

Soma Vida, a new shared work space in Austin, recently opened with a vision/goal rather similar to the original Spiral Muse vision. Soma Vida is a health and wellness center in East Austin, with coworking added on.

OfficeOps, in Brooklyn, works with a model similar to Spiral Muse and Soma Vida. It runs yoga and meditation classes alongside a coworking space.

More recently, Austin's **Conjunctured** now hosts yoga classes a couple of mornings a week with a guest instructor.

We would add that the world would be a healthier place if more people focused on achieving balance in their lives.

Are You on the Bus?

There's a generational stereotype about coworking.

Is coworking—both as a cultural movement and a style of working—primarily a Gen-Y/Millennial trend?

Nutopia's John McGann once suggested that: "The older generation comes in here and they just don't get it. Twenty five year olds don't need an explanation."

Yet, similar to the Cultural Revolution in the US in the late 1960s-early 1970s, people of all ages joined in the action. After all, Neil Cassady drove Ken Kesey and the Merry Pranksters across country in The Bus. Cassady was twice the age of most of the others on the bus, but they were all on the same trip.

While much of the drive and energy behind coworking's growth may derive from Millennials, people of all ages do get it. As the Merry Pranksters used to put it: "You're either on the bus or off."

 coworking   Search   Advance
                                                                              Preferen

Web   Blogs   Results **1 - 10**

Co-Working Space
www.Regus.com/Offices   Regus CoWorking Gives You Access To Offices, Lounges & Café
Worldwide.

NYC Coworking Space
www.SuiteMatch.com   Find shared office and coworking space. Simple, fast and free.

Sponsored Lin

Coworking / FrontPage
It is coworking with the two "o"s being zeroes! (Is this still true? wasn't that the wiki-wide invite
key which no longer exists? see above...) ...
coworking.pbwiki.com/ - 69k - Cached - Similar pages

CoworkingSanFrancisco	CoworkingSeattle
CoworkingAustin	CoworkingHouston
SpaceOwner	CoworkingChico
CoworkingBoston	CoworkingBarcelona

More results from pbwiki.com »

Coworking / SanFranciscoCoworking
Remote Office Centers - www.remoteofficecenters.com - Free web site for posting and searching
for Remote Offices. The site lists offices for coworking and ...
coworking.pbwiki.com/SanFranciscoCoworking - 24k - Cached - Similar pages

Coworking - Wikipedia, the free encyclopedia
Nov 10, 2008 ... Coworking is an emerging trend for a new pattern for working. Typically work-a

Bandwagon as Bellwether

If you Google "coworking," the first thing you see isn't Citizen Space, Hat Factory, Independents Hall, or any coworking space we've mentioned here.

Rather, it is Regus Office, the temp-office behemoth.

Dell's Digital Nomads

Anthropologists have long known that humans, at our core, are more nomadic than we are sedentary. Tools—scrapers, spears, bows, arrows, controlled-fire, hunting big game, telescopes, computers—enable us to leapfrog evolution time and again.

On any given day, millions of people are working outside of their "assigned offices." Teleworking, hoteling, on the road making a sale, whatever. This mobility is not lost on America's leading tech firms. Dell, for example, has recognized this new era of mobility and is listening to and designing tools for today's nomads.

DigitalNomads.com is a blog, a community, a conversation, a platform for this emerging global community of tech-enabled nomads.

The Dell Digital Nomads team scouts the world of today's nomads, trying to come up with the next generation of tools to make their work more productive.

Conclusion

While many of the people coworking today are freelancers and entrepreneurs, coworking is growing fast.

The Internet has fundamentally changed how we work. Advances in technology, particularly laptops and wireless connectivity, make it possible for people to work anywhere with a signal and an outlet.

The current recession is accelerating this change. In 2008, the United States suffered the most single-year job losses since 1945. More and more people, both voluntarily and involuntarily, are **leaving** the office.

All of this leads us to believe that more and more people will be joining the ranks of coworkers.

Learning about coworking over the course of the last year has been an incredibly exciting and educational experience for us, and we hope that this book has gotten you excited enough to check it out for yourself.

If there's no Jelly or Coworking community in your area, introduce yourself on the **Coworking Google Group**. Members of the group are helping new people get involved every day. Or check out the link below to our **Start A Coworking Community Cheatsheet**.

If you're stuck in an office job and still want to participate, there are many resources for working on getting out of the office. *The Four Hour Workweek* by Tim Ferriss and *Why Work Sucks and How to Fix It* by Cali

Ressler and Jody Thompson both offer great resources for getting out of the 9-to-5, whether by working with your employer or around them.

This book is simply a starting point. There is an ongoing conversation happening online now that you can participate in, and new coworking communities forming every day.

We'll see you there!

Read about all things coworking:
http://coworking.info

View coworking spaces worldwide:
http://tr.im/coworkingspacemap

Join the Coworking Google Group:
http://groups.google.com/group/coworking

Find a Jelly in your area:
http://workatjelly.com

Read our one-page cheat sheet for starting a coworking community:
http://imouttaherethebook.com/cheatsheets

Join the ongoing conversation:
http://imouttaherethebook.com

Leave feedback on the book and suggest additions:
http://imouttahere.uservoice.com

Drew Jones

Drew Jones is an anthropologist, management consultant, and former business school professor. He works with Shift101—an innovation agency with offices in Sydney, New York, and Austin-and writes and speaks about innovation, design, and the future of work.

Todd Sundsted

Todd has worked with and for companies big and small for twenty years, and has seen the best and the worst of contemporary organizational practice. His interest in coworking comes from his interest in innovation, and from his first hand experience with small, highly engaged teams and the incredible things they can accomplish. Todd is a entrepreneur, speaker, and published author; and he's wicked good with technology.

Tony Bacigalupo

Tony started and runs New Work City, a community coworking space in Manhattan. He is also a Project Manager at Desktop Solutions Software. Tony seeks to facilitate entrepreneurial growth and bring more balance to people's work lives in NYC.